THE NFL AT A GLANCE

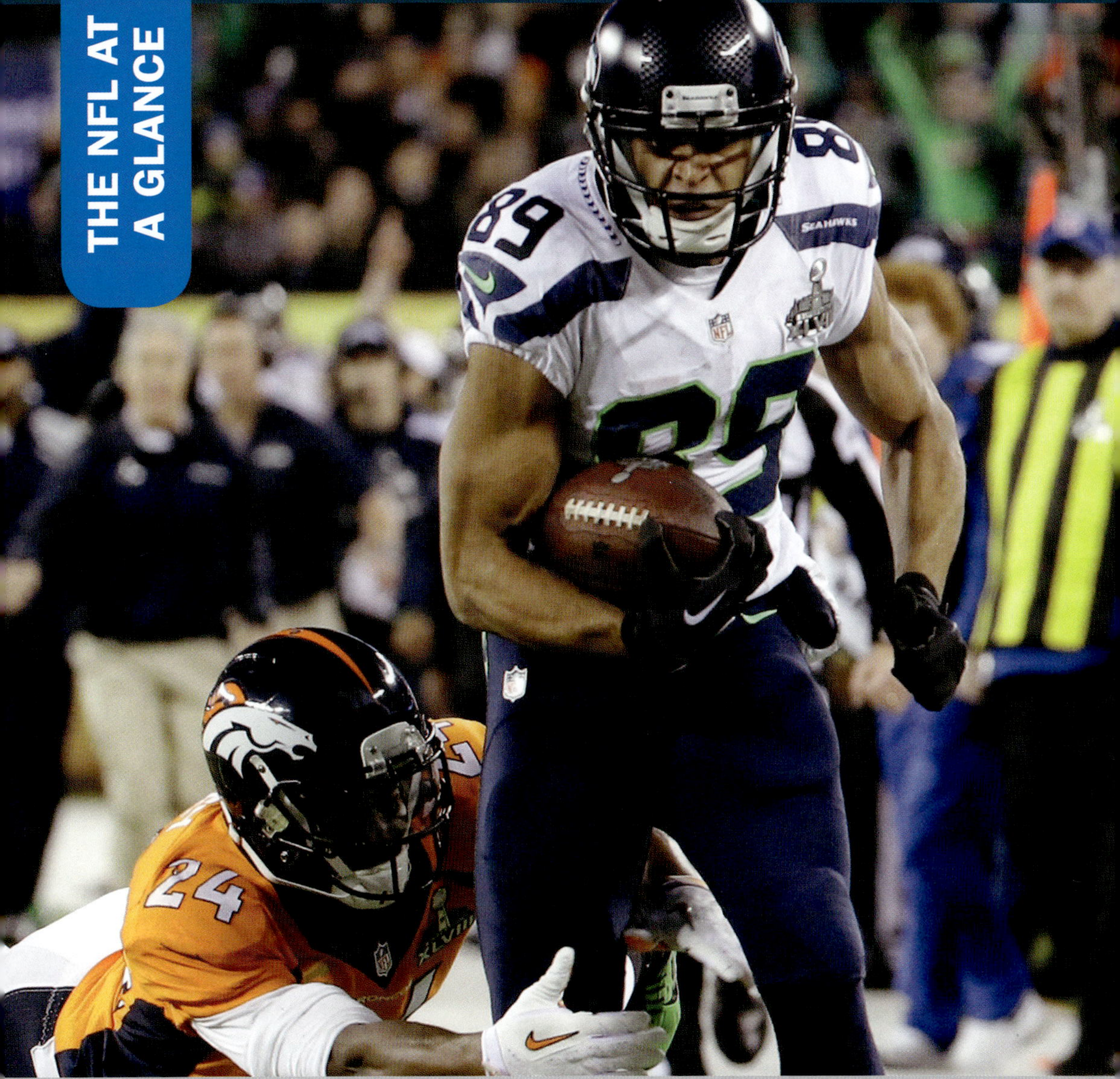

THE SUPER BOWL

12 REASONS TO LOVE THE NFL'S BIG GAME

by Drew Silverman

www.12StoryLibrary.com

12-Story Library is an imprint of Peterson Publishing Company and Press Room Editions.

Produced for 12-Story Library by Red Line Editorial

Photographs ©: Ted S. Warren/AP Images, cover, 1; Kathy Willens/AP Images, 5; AP Images, 6; Vernon Biever/AP Images, 7, 29; Gene Puskar/AP Images, 9; Scott Boehm/AP Images, 10; Paul Spinelli/AP Images, 13; Charlie Riedel/AP Images, 12; Ric Tapia/AP Images, 15, 18; PRNewsFoto/National Milk Mustache 'got milk?(R)' Campaign/AP Images, 16; Mark J. Terrill/AP Images, 19; Chris O'Meara/AP Images, 21; Tom DiPace/AP Images, 23, 28; John Gaps III/AP Images, 25; Al Messerschmidt/AP Images, 27

ISBN
978-1-63235-157-9 (hardcover)
978-1-63235-197-5 (paperback)
978-1-62143-249-4 (hosted ebook)

Library of Congress Control Number: 2015934302

Printed in the United States of America
Mankato, MN
June, 2015

TABLE OF CONTENTS

Upsets, Comebacks, and Drama Make for Amazing Action 4
Dynasties Are Born in the Big Game 6
Underdogs Shock the NFL's Powers 8
Super Bowl Sunday Becomes Must-Watch TV 10
Media Day Is a Circus Before the Super Bowl 12
Pregame Festivities Pump Up the Fans 14
Crazy Commercials Create Nonstop Fun 16
Halftime Is No Break at the Big Game 18
Amazing Seasons End in Heartbreak 20
The Super Bowl MVP Is the Star of the Show 22
Superstars Go Out on Top 24
Stars Become Legends in the Super Bowl 26
Fun Facts and Stories 28
Glossary 30
For More Information 31
Index 32
About the Author 32

1

UPSETS, COMEBACKS, AND DRAMA MAKE FOR AMAZING ACTION

Super Bowl Sunday is one of the most exciting days each year in sports. The Super Bowl features two teams playing for the National Football League (NFL) championship. Thousands of people watch the game from inside the stadium. Millions more watch on TV. For the players and coaches, everything is on the line. When the game lives up to the hype, the results are exciting. Many of the league's most memorable moments happened in the Super Bowl.

Super Bowl XLIX was one of those times. The game was in February 2015. It featured two powerhouse teams: the New England Patriots and the Seattle Seahawks.

Seattle led 24–21 in the fourth quarter. Then the Patriots came back. Quarterback Tom Brady led his team down the field for a touchdown. Now Seattle trailed 28–24. It was quarterback Russell Wilson's turn to shine. He led the Seahawks down to the 1-yard line. Only a minute remained. A touchdown would likely win the game. But the Seahawks did not score. Instead, Patriots rookie Malcolm Butler intercepted Wilson's pass to seal the win.

6

Super Bowls Tom Brady and the Patriots played in from the 2001 to 2014 seasons.

- New England won four of those Super Bowls.
- All six of those games were decided in the final two minutes.

New England Patriots cornerback Malcolm Butler makes an interception. His play saved Super Bowl XLIX.

2

DYNASTIES ARE BORN IN THE BIG GAME

Great teams win one Super Bowl. Dynasties keep on winning them.

The Green Bay Packers were the first Super Bowl dynasty. They won the NFL championship in 1965. Then they won the first two Super Bowls. Those were held after the 1966 and 1967 seasons.

Many legendary teams followed the Packers. The Pittsburgh Steelers stood out. They won four Super Bowls between the 1974 and 1979 seasons. The San Francisco 49ers took over in the 1980s. They won four in that decade. Next came the Dallas Cowboys. That team won three titles in four years in the 1990s.

The Pittsburgh Steelers' Lynn Swann makes a diving catch in Super Bowl X in January 1976. The Steelers beat the Dallas Cowboys.

Quarterback Joe Montana led the San Francisco 49ers to four Super Bowl wins.

The NFL kept growing. It reached 32 teams in 2002. Winning multiple titles became harder than ever. Yet the New England Patriots proved to be a modern-day dynasty. They have been the most successful team since 2000. New England won the Super Bowls after the 2001, 2003, 2004, and 2014 seasons. The Patriots also appeared in two others.

46

NFL seasons before the first Super Bowl was held in January 1967. The league began in 1920.

- The American Football League (AFL) debuted in 1960 to rival the NFL.
- The first Super Bowls featured the AFL and NFL champions.
- The NFL and AFL joined together to form one league in 1970.

BEST OF THE BEST

The Pittsburgh Steelers won Super Bowl XLIII after the 2008 season. It was the team's record sixth title. Two teams have five. They are the Dallas Cowboys and San Francisco 49ers. The Green Bay Packers, New England Patriots, and New York Giants have won four each. Twenty-three teams have reached multiple Super Bowls. Of them, only the Baltimore Ravens are undefeated, at 2–0.

3

UNDERDOGS SHOCK THE NFL'S POWERS

Some Super Bowls have pretty evenly matched teams. Sometimes, though, one team is a huge favorite. But that team doesn't always win. Just ask the New England Patriots.

The Patriots were huge underdogs in the 2001 season. Quarterback Tom Brady was young and unproven. Meanwhile, no one doubted the St. Louis Rams' skill. Their amazing offense was nicknamed "The Greatest Show on Turf." Yet the two teams ended up against each other in Super Bowl XXXVI. And the Patriots won 20–17 on the final play.

Six years later, New England was a powerhouse. The Patriots hadn't lost all year. Most experts predicted they would win their last game, too. The New York Giants didn't seem to stand a chance in Super Bowl XLII. Then the impossible happened. The Patriots led just 14–10 in the fourth quarter. Giants quarterback Eli Manning then threw a long, desperate pass. Little-known receiver David Tyree was there. He caught the ball against his helmet while falling to the ground. Four plays later, Manning threw the winning touchdown pass. The upset was complete.

18

Games in a row the Patriots had won before losing to the Giants in Super Bowl XLII.

- The Patriots were only the second team in the Super Bowl era to win every regular-season game.
- The 2007 Giants went 10–6 and barely made the playoffs.
- David Tyree had just four catches in the entire 2007 regular season.

The New York Giants' David Tyree catches the ball against his helmet in Super Bowl XLII.

A GUARANTEED UPSET

The first big upset in Super Bowl history came in Super Bowl III. The Baltimore Colts faced the New York Jets. The well-established Colts were expected to win easily. Yet Joe Namath had other plans. The Jets' young quarterback guaranteed a victory three days before the game. On Super Bowl Sunday, he backed up his words. Namath passed for 206 yards. The Jets won 16–7.

4

SUPER BOWL SUNDAY BECOMES MUST-WATCH TV

Americans love to watch football. Regular-season games get huge TV ratings. In fact, the most-watched show each week is often an NFL game. But those ratings go through the roof for the Super Bowl. After all, the game is not just the championship of the United States' most popular sports league. It also features star-studded halftime shows and many creative, new commercials.

More than 100 million people tune in to the big game every year in the United States. It's almost always the most-watched show of the year. And the most-watched shows ever are mostly Super Bowls. Super Bowl XLVIII was held after the 2013 season. A record 112 million people watched in the United States. That record only lasted a year. More than 114 million US viewers watched the next year's Super Bowl.

A TV camera films Super Bowl XLVIII in February 2014.

THINK ABOUT IT

Only two teams can play in the Super Bowl. Yet fans from all over the United States always tune in. Why do you think people are so interested in the big game?

After that, seven of the eight most-watched shows in US history were Super Bowls.

Plus, technology is changing the way people watch the Super Bowl. They no longer have to be by a TV to see it. Instead fans can stream the game over their computer or phone.

180

Different countries in which the Super Bowl is broadcast.

- The Super Bowl is broadcast in 34 languages.
- A record 28.4 million tweets were related to Super Bowl XLIX in February 2015.
- In Seattle, 89 percent of TVs on during the Super Bowl were tuned in to the big game (but the hometown Seahawks lost).

PUPPY BOWL

TV networks understand that most viewers on Super Bowl Sunday prefer to watch the game. However, a few networks try to compete with the game, even if just for fun. Animal Planet debuted *Puppy Bowl* in February 2005. It features puppies playing together on a mini football field. The "game" also has a "Kitty Halftime Show." An amazing 13.5 million people watched part of the 12-hour broadcast in February 2014. During that year's Super Bowl game, *Puppy Bowl* averaged 3.3 million viewers.

5

MEDIA DAY IS A CIRCUS BEFORE THE SUPER BOWL

The Super Bowl is not just on Sunday. Teams arrive in the host city a week before the game. And with the teams comes the media. Super Bowl XLIX was held after the 2014 season. More than 2,000 media members from around the world showed up. They came from newspapers, magazines, websites, and TV and radio stations. And they all wanted something to report on.

The NFL makes sure that is not a problem. Media Day is the Tuesday before the Super Bowl. All of the players and head coaches come to answer questions. Many of the questions are serious. Reporters ask their typical questions about

Reporters crowd around Seattle Seahawks quarterback Russell Wilson at Media Day for Super Bowl XLIX in January 2015.

2

TV networks that aired Super Bowl XLIX Media Day live.

- The NFL sells tickets so fans can attend Media Day.
- Fans can't always hear the players, so they can listen to the interviews on a radio.

THINK ABOUT IT

The NFL requires that players meet with reporters. This rule helps the media cover the league. However, not all players enjoy talking to the media. Sometimes they protest. For example, the Seattle Seahawks' Marshawn Lynch once answered every question the same. Do you think it's fair that players are required to talk to the media? Are the players who protest being fair to reporters, who have their own job to do?

strategy for the game or about the players' backstories. But sometimes Media Day gets wacky.

New England Patriots tight end Rob Gronkowski was a hit at Super Bowl XLIX Media Day. He sang for one reporter. He made jokes. Another reporter asked "Gronk" his favorite number. The Patriots' star chose No. 87—the number on the back of his jersey. Other times the media members are the goofy ones. Some have arrived in bizarre outfits. They have dressed as movie characters or superheroes. Either way, the event is sure to be a circus.

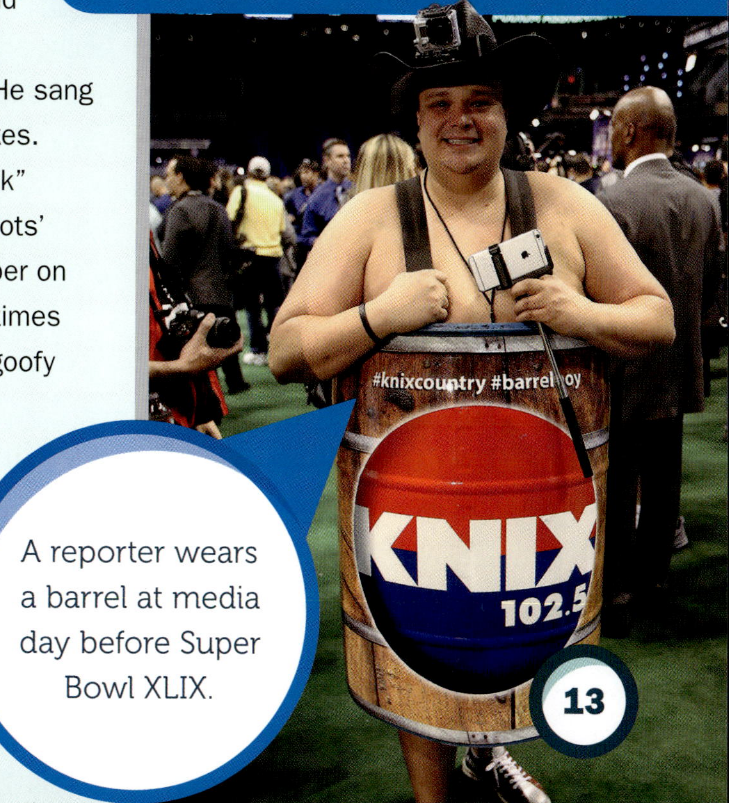

A reporter wears a barrel at media day before Super Bowl XLIX.

6

PREGAME FESTIVITIES PUMP UP THE FANS

The Super Bowl kicks off around 6:30 p.m. on the East Coast of the United States. However, the pregame TV shows begin long before that. Most Super Bowl pregame shows start in the morning. They last for several hours. These shows feature experts. Many times they are former players and coaches. The experts analyze the matchup. They discuss topics such as strategy, and each team's strengths and weaknesses. This helps get fans ready for the Super Bowl.

As the game gets closer, the pregame entertainment takes place at the stadium. Each year, a celebrity sings "America the Beautiful" on the field shortly before the opening kickoff. Then, another celebrity sings "The Star Spangled Banner." Often, military jets fly over the stadium just before the game, too.

The final activity before the Super Bowl is the coin toss. The referee flips a coin. One player calls "heads" or "tails." If the player guesses right, his team gets to decide who starts the game with the football. Once the pregame shows are completed, the songs have been sung, and the coin has been flipped, it's finally time for football.

346

Hours of NFL coverage on the ESPN networks in the week before Super Bowl XLIX after the 2014 season.

- John Legend sang "America the Beautiful" before Super Bowl XLIX.
- Idina Menzel sang the national anthem.

US Air Force jets fly over the stadium just before Super Bowl XLIX kicked off in February 2015.

VIEWING OPTIONS

Only one TV network is allowed to broadcast the Super Bowl each year. That doesn't stop other networks from covering the game, though. Super Bowl XLVIII officially began at 6 p.m. on February 2, 2014. The NFL Network began pregame coverage at 7 a.m. that morning. ESPN started at 10 a.m. Fox, which broadcast the game, began its pregame coverage at noon. President Obama did an interview on Fox before the game, too.

7

CRAZY COMMERCIALS CREATE NONSTOP FUN

The Super Bowl gets huge TV audiences. More than 100 million people watch every year. For advertisers, that means a lot of potential customers. So companies spend big bucks to buy Super Bowl commercial time. In 2015, a 30-second commercial during Super Bowl XLIX cost $4.5 million.

Actor Dwayne "The Rock" Johnson works on a Super Bowl commercial in 2013.

The advertisers don't waste the opportunity. They often create special ads just for the Super Bowl. Sometimes they are funny. Sometimes they try to make people think deeper about an issue. No matter what, though, companies want them to be memorable.

One of the most famous Super Bowl ads was in 1984. It showed a woman in athletic clothes running with a sledgehammer. She then threw the hammer at a giant screen. At the end, the ad announced that Apple's new Macintosh computer would be released soon. Other companies are known for regularly advertising at the Super Bowl. They include Pepsi, Doritos, and adult beverage companies.

Companies have tried to get more creative with their Super Bowl ads. Now many fans watch the big game just to see the commercials.

$30 million

Amount Anheuser-Busch spent to buy 210 seconds of ad time in Super Bowl XLIX.

- Some companies now offer previews of their commercials before the Super Bowl. This helps create more buzz.
- Many ads are uploaded to the Internet after the game, too.

WHAT GAME?

Some people watch the Super Bowl just for the commercials. One cable TV company had an idea. It has a device for recording TV. One feature on the device allows viewers to skip the commercials. A new feature was added for Super Bowl XLIX. Instead, viewers could skip through the game and just watch commercials.

8

HALFTIME IS NO BREAK AT THE BIG GAME

NFL games usually have a 12-minute halftime. The Super Bowl halftime is roughly twice that long. That allows the league to put on another show.

Today's halftime shows are huge productions. Famous musicians take center stage. Light shows, dancers, and special effects make the shows extra impressive. A crew even quickly builds a stage in the middle of the field just for the show.

Many music stars have performed at the Super Bowl. They include modern pop stars such as Beyoncé, Bruno Mars, Justin Timberlake, and Katy Perry. Classic acts such as the Rolling Stones, Paul McCartney, and U2 have performed, too. One of the most famous halftimes was in February 2007. Prince played seven songs. One was his hit "Purple Rain." Real rain fell on the stadium as he played.

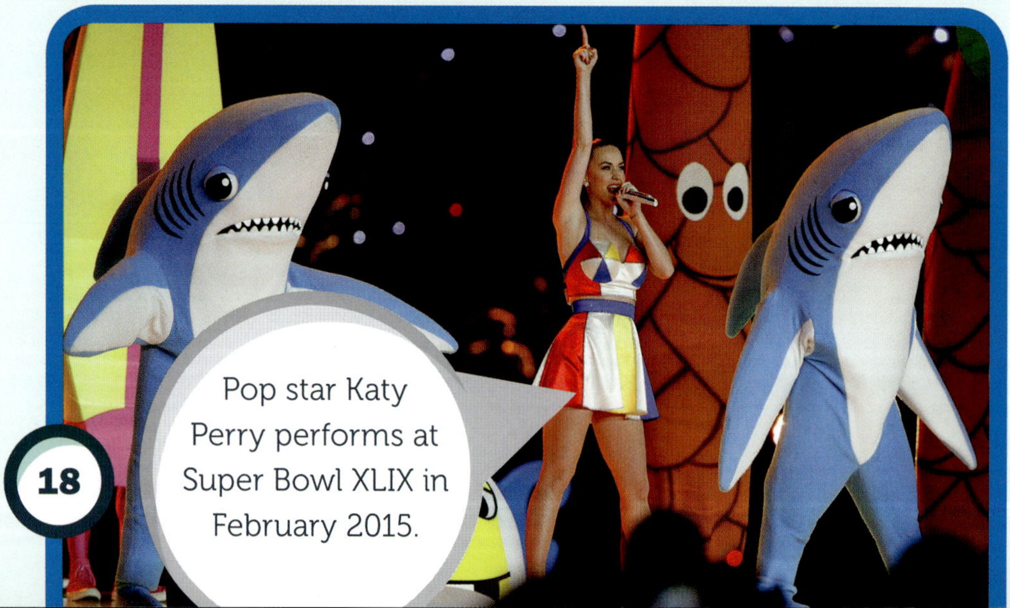

Pop star Katy Perry performs at Super Bowl XLIX in February 2015.

Halftime shows weren't always star-studded events. Early Super Bowls often featured marching bands or skits at halftime. In fact, a high school marching band played at halftime of Super Bowl I after the 1966 season.

Prince at Super Bowl XLI in February 2007.

The trend changed in January 1993. Pop icon Michael Jackson took the stage at Super Bowl XXVII. The "King of Pop" performed in front of nearly 100,000 fans at the Rose Bowl in Pasadena, California. That set the trend of having superstars at the Super Bowl.

12

Minutes, approximately, that performers have on stage in a Super Bowl halftime show.

- A crew also has to build and take down a stage between the second and third quarters.
- Sometimes a select group of fans is allowed onto the field to watch the show.

THINK ABOUT IT

Musicians are typically paid to perform concerts. That might not be the case at future Super Bowls. The Super Bowl attracts a huge audience. It is good publicity for the musicians. So the NFL has considered asking artists to pay for the opportunity to play. Do you think this is fair? Why or why not?

9

AMAZING SEASONS END IN HEARTBREAK

The Super Bowl era began with the 1966 season. Since then, no team has had a run quite like the Buffalo Bills. From 1990 to 1993, they won 13, 13, 11, and 12 games. And each year they reached the Super Bowl. The heartbreak started right away, though. Super Bowl XXV was after the 1990 season. The Bills were favored to beat the New York Giants by approximately one touchdown.

New York led 20–19 with a little more than two minutes left. But the Bills' star quarterback, Jim Kelly, led a ferocious drive. Buffalo moved 61 yards down the field. The team got as far as the Giants' 29-yard line. With eight seconds left, kicker Scott Norwood came on. If he made the 47-yard field goal, the Bills would win. But he missed. The ball sailed wide right of the uprights.

It was only the beginning for Buffalo fans. The Washington Redskins beat Buffalo in the next Super Bowl. Then the Dallas Cowboys beat the Bills twice in a row. Through the 2014 season, Buffalo still had not won a Super Bowl. But the Bills remained the only team to have made four Super Bowls in a row.

4

NFL teams that had never played in a Super Bowl through the 2014 season.

- They are the Cleveland Browns, Detroit Lions, Jacksonville Jaguars, and Houston Texans.
- The Browns and Lions both won NFL titles in the pre–Super Bowl era.
- The Jaguars began playing in 1995 and the Texans in 2002.

Other teams have suffered similar Super Bowl heartbreak. The Minnesota Vikings reached four Super Bowls from the 1969 to 1976 seasons. Yet they lost all four. The Denver Broncos also lost their first four Super Bowls. That streak ran from the 1977 to 1989 seasons. Denver was able to shed that losing legacy, though. The Broncos won two titles in a row after the 1997 and 1998 seasons.

Buffalo Bills kicker Scott Norwood walks off the field after missing a field goal that would have won Super Bowl XXV in January 1991.

10

THE SUPER BOWL MVP IS THE STAR OF THE SHOW

It takes a great team to reach a Super Bowl. To win a Super Bowl often takes an extraordinary performance. The NFL honors the best individual performance with the Super Bowl Most Valuable Player (MVP) Award.

Some of the NFL's all-time greats have been the MVP. San Francisco 49ers quarterback Joe Montana won it three times. He threw 11 touchdown passes and zero interceptions in his four Super Bowl wins. The New England Patriots' Tom Brady tied Montana with four championships and three MVPs. He won his third MVP Award in Super Bowl XLIX after the 2014 season. Brady led a game-winning drive in the fourth quarter in all three Super Bowls in which he was named MVP. Other great players honored as Super Bowl MVP include Jerry Rice, John Elway, Ray Lewis, and Peyton Manning.

Yet MVPs aren't always superstars. Few had heard of Malcolm Smith before Super Bowl XLVIII. Then the Seattle Seahawks' linebacker had a game for the ages. He had nine tackles and recovered a fumble. But he is best remembered for his 69-yard interception return for a

27

Times in which a quarterback has been named Super Bowl MVP through Super Bowl XLIX.

- Running backs are the second most common MVPs with seven.
- Nine defensive players and one kick returner have been MVPs.

touchdown. Wide receiver Deion Branch never made a Pro Bowl. But he had 11 catches for 143 yards and a touchdown in Super Bowl XXXVIII. That helped the Patriots win their third Super Bowl in four years.

Tom Brady was Super Bowl MVP in three of his four wins with the New England Patriots.

11

SUPERSTARS GO OUT ON TOP

There is no greater prize in pro football than a Super Bowl title. Players spend their careers working toward this goal. Most never achieve it. Even many superstars fall short.

John Elway appeared on that path. The Denver Broncos' quarterback was one of the best in the NFL. But he had a bad record in the Super Bowl. The Broncos reached the game three times in the late 1980s. All three times they lost. That finally changed in the 1997 season. Elway was 37 and nearing the end of his career. Finally, in Super Bowl XXXII, his Broncos won. Then Elway came back for one more season in 1998. And he led his team to victory again.

Jerome Bettis had a similar story. He was a bruising running back for the Pittsburgh Steelers. For nine seasons, the Steelers were usually good—just not good enough. Finally, in his 10th season in Pittsburgh, they broke through. The Steelers won Super Bowl XL in February 2006.

Superstar middle linebacker Ray Lewis had won one Super Bowl with the Baltimore Ravens. In February 2013, at age 37, he won another. Lewis retired after that.

15

Seasons defensive end Michael Strahan played before winning a Super Bowl in his final season.

- Strahan and his New York Giants won Super Bowl XLII after the 2007 season.
- Ray Lewis and the Ravens won their first Super Bowl after the 2000 season.

"It is the most ultimate feeling ever," Lewis said after the Super Bowl. "This is the way you do it. No other way to go out and end a career. This is how you do it."

THINK ABOUT IT

Put yourself in the shoes of an NFL veteran. Pretend you had played 13 seasons and your team won a Super Bowl in your 13th season. Would you retire as a champion? Or would you come back the next season to try for another championship, knowing you might fall short?

Denver Broncos quarterback John Elway celebrates after winning Super Bowl XXXIII in January 1999.

12

STARS BECOME LEGENDS IN THE SUPER BOWL

There is no bigger stage in American sports than the Super Bowl. Players who excel there go down in history.

Joe Montana was known for being calm. Playing under pressure rarely rattled him. That helped him become the NFL's most successful quarterback in the 1980s. Montana led the San Francisco 49ers to four Super Bowl wins. That was a record for most wins by a quarterback until 2015. Then Tom Brady led his New England Patriots to a fourth Super Bowl title. Neither quarterback was considered the most talented of his era. But because they won so many Super Bowls, they reached an extra level of fame.

Many players have become legends due to their Super Bowl performances. Adam Vinatieri kicked game-winning field goals for the Patriots twice. St. Louis Rams linebacker Mike Jones made a tackle at the 1-yard line to secure Super Bowl XXXIV in January 2000. The Pittsburgh Steelers trailed the Arizona Cardinals late in Super Bowl XLIII in February 2009. Wide receiver Santonio Holmes snatched a touchdown catch in the corner of the end zone. Pittsburgh won 27–23.

92

Yards Joe Montana led the 49ers in 11 plays late in Super Bowl XXIII after the 1988 season.

- The 49ers trailed the Cincinnati Bengals 16–13.
- Montana completed the game-winning touchdown pass to John Taylor with 34 seconds left.

San Francisco 49ers quarterback Joe Montana passes the ball in Super Bowl XXIII in January 1989.

THE OTHER SIDE

Peyton Manning is an amazing passer. He holds many records. After 16 seasons, he had won five NFL MVP Awards. By many measures, Manning is the best quarterback of all time. Yet there is great debate among fans. That's because Manning has struggled in the playoffs. He played in three Super Bowls but won only one of them. He threw more interceptions than touchdown passes in those games.

FUN FACTS AND STORIES

- Atlanta Falcons cornerback Ray Buchanan made headlines at Super Bowl Media Day in 1999. He called Denver Broncos star Shannon Sharpe "ugly" and added that he "looks like a horse." Sharpe and the Broncos got the last laugh three days later. They defeated the Falcons 34–19.

- Thanksgiving is the day when the most food is consumed in the United States. Super Bowl Sunday is second. One of the most popular foods at Super Bowl parties is chicken wings. The National Chicken Council estimates that fans ate 1.25 billion chicken wings during Super Bowl XLIX in February 2015.

- "I remember my dad asking me one time, and it's something that has always stuck with me: 'Why not you, Russ?' You know, why not me? Why not me in the Super Bowl?" —Russell Wilson made the Super Bowl in his second NFL season. He led the Seattle Seahawks to a 43–8 victory over legendary quarterback Peyton Manning and the Denver Broncos.

- For years, there was no known video footage of Super Bowl I. Two networks showed the game. But both taped over their original footage. CBS taped a soap opera over the footage of the Green Bay Packers defeating the Kansas City Chiefs. However, in 2005, a man emerged with CBS footage of much of the game. His father had been an engineer at a local TV station.

GLOSSARY

dynasty
A team that wins several championships over a short period of time.

favorite
A team that is expected to win.

hype
Excessive publicity and commotion surrounding a person or event.

legacy
The way an athlete is remembered after leaving a team or a sport.

media
People who work in the mass communication industry, such as at newspapers, TV stations, or websites.

publicity
Attention given to somebody or something from the media.

ratings
Numbers based on a sample that indicate what percentage of the potential audience is tuned in to a particular program.

retire
To officially end one's career.

rookie
A first-year player.

upset
An unexpected result or outcome.

FOR MORE INFORMATION

Books

Hetrick, Hans. *The Super Bowl: All About Pro Football's Biggest Event.* Mankato, MN: Capstone Press, 2012.

McGinn, Bob. *The Ultimate Super Bowl Book*. Minneapolis, MN: MVP Books, 2012.

Wilner, Barry. *The Super Bowl.* Minneapolis, MN: Abdo Publishing, 2013.

Websites

NFL Rush

www.nflrush.com

Pro Football Hall of Fame

www.profootballhof.com

Pro Football Reference

www.pro-football-reference.com

Sports Illustrated Kids

www.sikids.com

INDEX

Arizona Cardinals, 26

Baltimore Colts, 9
Baltimore Ravens, 7, 24
Bettis, Jerome, 24
Brady, Tom, 4, 8, 22, 26
Branch, Deion, 23
Buffalo Bills, 20
Butler, Malcolm, 4

Dallas Cowboys, 6–7, 20
Denver Broncos, 21, 24

Elway, John, 22, 24

Green Bay Packers, 6–7
Gronkowski, Rob, 13

Holmes, Santonio, 26

Jackson, Michael, 19
Jones, Mike, 26

Kelly, Jim, 20

Lewis, Ray, 22, 24–25

Manning, Eli, 8
Manning, Peyton, 22, 27
Media Day, 12–13
Minnesota Vikings, 21
Montana, Joe, 22, 26

Namath, Joe, 9
New England Patriots, 4, 7, 8, 13, 22–23, 26
New York Giants, 7, 8, 20
New York Jets, 9
Norwood, Scott, 20

Pittsburgh Steelers, 6–7, 24, 26
Puppy Bowl, 11

Rice, Jerry, 22

San Francisco 49ers, 6–7, 22, 26
Seattle Seahawks, 4, 22
Smith, Malcolm, 22
St. Louis Rams, 8, 26

TV, 4, 10–11, 12, 14–15, 16–17
Tyree, David, 8

Vinatieri, Adam, 26

Washington Redskins, 20
Wilson, Russell, 4

About the Author

Drew Silverman is a sportswriter based in Philadelphia. He graduated from Syracuse University and has worked for ESPN, Comcast SportsNet, and NBC Sports. He also was sports editor of *The Bulletin* newspaper in Philadelphia. He lives in Philadelphia with his wife and his son.